CARIBBEAN PASSION

Some of these poems have appeared in the following magazines and journals:

The Caribbean Writer; *Obsidian III*; *Xavier Review*; *MaComère, Isis Rising & Ruptures;* and in *Gifts from our Grandmothers,* edited by Carol Dovi (Crown Publishers) 2000

Dedicated to Orville & Nigel

CARIBBEAN PASSION

OPAL PALMER ADISA

PEEPAL TREE

First published in Great Britain in 2004
Peepal Tree Press Ltd
17 King's Avenue
Leeds LS6 1QS
UK

ISBN 1 900715 92 9

 Peepal Tree gratefully acknowledges Arts Council support

CONTENTS

AN ARAWAK SPEAKS

for the record

it was not
with innocent eyes
i   the indigenous
of these shores
watched
your arrival

your coming
was long prophesied

> *often when scaling*
> *a fish its gill*
> *will bleed your fingers*

i'll always
be here

if you doubt me
place your ear
to the ground

> *the moon's fullness*
> *blinds the sun*
> *but cannot deny*
> *its existence*

TIDE TURN

the warm breath of
the caribbean sea
laps at my feet

did your eyes
   your tongue
   your guns
   your bible
               speak?
no need to answer

it answered for you
taking into its mouth
your discarded condom
evidence of your betrayal

you will not hear me howl
like hurricane winds
strangling palm fronds
and ripping trees
from their rooting

debauchery was
the site of our meeting
but
i will not be
your whore

1865 BRUK-UP

thud   thud   thud
the endless dirge of
shovel against rock
gravel too marl
to bed seed
too salt
to strengthen roots

paul minding them business
mouth twisting how to frame
them demands
when the earth spoke
pick up de bible in yu right hand
and them struggle in yu left

from way yonder
them marching
machetes perched on their shoulders
tip pointed backwards
and is now he take up
their woes like wasp nest

i know why it name
stony gut
no family can feed
from the mawga ribs
of a hillside
the land hard
like dry coconut
that's what i go tell them

45 miles to spanish town
he trekked
his words
like lacatan banana
that melt in the mouth
but dem tun deaf ears

he come back
with a swollen tongue

400 strong with him
them faces yellow yam
them march to morant bay
crying food   water
not even phlegm
the soil can cough up
but soldiers chase and beat them
so dem bun de court house down
right to the ground
bogle put down the bible
and pick up de struggle in both hands

bogle in the thick of things
and the voice still say
go on man   press on
his friend g w gordon
chatting for them too
so dem hang him

bogle wake one october morning
with dry throat
he did know and he didn't know
not even when the rope caressed
his neck

430 slaughtered with him
their anger caught in flames
1000 homes burnt
before them sorrow mek news

oh morant bay   thud
lawd paul bogle   thud
wow morant bay   thud

rock-stone drink blood

HISTORY

memory
it is said
must be buried like the dead
if burned
the ash could serve
as evidence and
who wants to be reminded of the past

we did not look back
shame was the language of exchange
like ganja soaking in rum
it was hidden in the back of the medicine cabinet

forgive
but the bones keep appearing
everywhere

africa is a tenacious weed

INDIGENOUS

(for bert neapaulsing)

we grew beneath the sea
to soar mountains
7000 strong
once we were ourselves

heartlands of flowers
nations of birthrights
we held the ocean
in the bowl of our palms

we were shallow waters
guanahani   not bahamas
children diamonded in the ocean
under the noonday sun

fat crocodiles sauntered
on the sand
not caymans
money laundering

when quisqueya lost her army
no longer mother or nation
she was divided deep
sold as the dominican republic

and what of camerhogue
where the ocean chops
refashioned as another's self
invaded grenada

oh seething beautiful waters
i hear your chant   *karukera karukera*
guadeloupe is a quacksalver
counterfeit of france

xaymaca where are you
in jamaica?
the arawaks knew you
as land of wood and water

madinina   your fragrant petals
hidden in martinique
stand close to alliougana
prickly bush wedded montserrat

unsheathe your swords
brave lords
what shall we call you
puerto rico or buriquen?

iouanalao or hewannorra
was a fitting name
for the land of iguanas
where no st lucia ever lived

st martin/st maarten
twins pulled from the womb
your salted plain
was once soualiga

iere was the freedom call
of the humming bird
hovering in a Trinidad
rechristened for another's faith

before she was poisoned as st kitts
anegada napped
like a turtle
in the ocean

but haiti i hail you
in the mountainous land
freedom's first torch
you alone kept your name

so travel homeward
i need you to remember
that blessed st vincent
used to be hairoun

that she will tell you stories
buried in the navel of the ocean
the crabs will retrieve them
you will make them known

chainless but chained
we are bastardized flags
sinking in the ocean
mapped by the triangular trade

crabs in a barrel
clawing at sovereignty we cry
this is my name
this is my name

RUN-AWAY BAY

me left
wearing de sun
as a broad-rimmed hat

me soles caked in yolk
lime juice rubbed
into me armpits

me neva smell
de fear on me back
only de cane-juice
dat run down me legs
before him vanished
into a night when
de breeze had amnesia

sometimes yu feet ave eyes
every run away
nuh maroon
me walked
as if memory
was de road
and me knew where
desire was tekin me

it didn't name so
until me came dere
find others
tree and chicken
shelter and food
duppy know who fi frighten
me gwane like me deaf
de bay conceal me

one day
a touch gwane mek
him find me
time longa dan rope
but until mango fall off tree
me eyes hypnotize by de sea
cane trash frothing
in de waves
and me foot know
lumps of salt

MILK-RIVER

afta dem tek me child
me swear on me womb

no more
not anoda blasted one

ten years
ten rass years

not one of we
not one

give birth
we turn dem back

turn all a dem back
we women punishin we wombs

titties
engorged

milk   tamarind vinegar
pus blistering de nipples

den saline water
cause a mud-slide

de pain flowed out
spilling into de earth

mekin a path for itself
for me self

fi bathe me loss
and go on

milky river
healing

DISCOVERY BAY

me neva really knew
who me was carrying
around wid me

suh me run again
not from de truth
but de bearing up unda
me alone left wid
dis child in me belly
and mama cripple

every time me sidown
turquoise ground
lizard run ova me foot
and shadow shawls
me back like big fence

she live
but de four still born
hitch-up in de back of me belly
de wall between
forgiveness
and hope

one a dem tell me
look in de mirror
read me heart

me eyes dance
jus lookin pan she

how me fi know
dats wha me ask meself
how me fi know

dem chop off her sixth finger
and dash it gi dog
dem say she mark
she whose face clean like rain

me eyes gwane
like two left foot pan dance-floor

me neva ask fi dis
me neva wan dis burial heap
me children dust in de earth

de bay open
right in de middle
of de sea
and wata wing me hand

HOPE GARDENS

de moment me cross ova
me step pan croton
and smell stale piss

is mus mistake dis
me seh kissin me teeth
walkin in a yard
swept clean and lonely
old can lids hung from trees
twirlin and clangin
de sheet pan de line
blowin in de midday breeze
den me see
de yam heads piled
by de kitchen door

eheh
someting nuh right
sometimes yu ahfi swallow
yu tongue and mek
jackass walk in front ah yu
suh me nuh complain

me hear de children
singin down by de gully
dem voice fresh roasted peanut

same place me stop
cock me head
her name ringin in me ears

yu mus visit
de obeah oman
when de moon is an arch

enter her house
backwards
salt in yu left palm

memba
nuh answer in de dark
yu name nuh wrap in garlic

JUSTICE

he leans against the wall
a hot red-stripe beer
held in front of his crotch

his body rocks to the rhythm
radar eyes scan the dance floor

she fits in his mind
as snugly as a mouse in a trap

he feasts on her gyrating sways
he knows she knows
he's devouring her

rawtid
he mumbles
as vibration surges his body
what a slack woman
justice is

LIVING

is easy enough
if you can forget
what you will do tomorrow

my grandmother died
and was buried in jamaica
my father didn't attend the funeral
he hasn't been home in thirty years

a severed wound

thirteen stitches

my foot went through
the bicycle spokes
as he pedaled

my mother warned him
about riding me on the handle bar

it's not that
i won't forget
memory is as a weed
struggling through concrete

JERK

buried in the earth-oven
one learns to measure speech
where to place the feet
to avoid burning

and when my children pull at me
to hold up their lives
i remember my mother's maxim
time longer than rope
and add my own
this too shall pass

at bumpy grave
where nanny remains lie
a heroine comes to us
intact like our hands
washed clean in rain water

seasoning sweetens pork
pepper cures
they made the march
all three hundred
going and coming
crossing the mountain range
for freedom
better to die than surrender

such a people cannot fail

tek yu time eat it nuh

MOLASSES

i'm a hands woman
love to take his large fingers
and suck on the tip of each one
just before i walk away

molasses is that audacious
once you use it to sweeten your tea
you'll never go back to sugar
but beware
it sticks to everything
leaving a trail

molasses can be callous
leave it to harden
and you'll pass each other on the street
your hatred all that connects you
not even remembering
the lunch time quickies
that got you through
the afternoon of work

mark my words
children who turn away
from their parents
will not have the pleasure
of sitting at a table
spread in their honor

family is kindred
to molasses

PEANUT

the shortest distance between
a ripe cocoa pod
and a tamarind
is the seed you must spit out

whenever you listening
to big people story
yu must mek yuself small-small
and be quiet-quiet
or the confusion of adults
will give you a headache

with october rains
the river swells her belly
and even the most holy believer
turns around and asks god
why cane so sweet
but reaping it so hard

but choking on peanut
is no laughing matter
you could cough out your insides
before you dislodge it
and by then your brassiere will be off
and his hand on the small of your back
will open to enfold you

impulse is
that sweet

LIME

green remembers
the taste of bitterness
as daddy walked by
with his sweetheart

it was cho-cho
the name for your
little-girl-private-parts
that you were told
to cover up

it was the man by the outhouse
holding his penis
and beckoning to you

it was the tension in your stomach
the evening before
the scholarship results
appeared in the *gleaner*

green was not knowing
what to say or how to feel
when the boy you liked
picked your bud breast
during the ring game

and waking to find
your panties soaked
with blood

but there's nothing to compare
with roast breadfruit in the morning

POINSETTIA

red was always a fickle color
but who cared when the mad woman
screamed off her head

or your mother didn't speak to you
and the words you needed
ran off and left you stranded

red could be capricious all she wants
that doesn't alter the beauty of hibiscus
or make them any less useful for
shining shoes

dangerous or bold
as women sitting legs spread
using their skirts to fan the heat
between their thighs
or peppered shrimp
soliciting water from your eyes

red is that mean sometimes

ACKEE

carefully remove
de red membrane
before cooking

> *if yu nyam de fish too fast*
> *bone gwane choke yu*

wash then steam
seasoned with salt-fish and onions
eat with johnny-cake and boiled green banana

> *laugh yu belly laugh*
> *an fall off de chair*
> *yu belly in stitches*

beware
the jeers of strange men on the street
that cause your feet to stumble

*Ackee is Jamaica's national dish, but if picked and eaten too early
is poisonous.

POUI

yellow is decidedly hot
like curried goat simmered with pepper
or jumping-rope to the rhythm of
your desire's name

it's love bush covering
everything it clings to
like wormy fingers
crawling up your legs
and you not knowing
how to say stop
or even if you want to say stop
or how to pretend as if
it's not awakening something
somewhere inside you

you cannot draw a line
between guinep and june-plum
or jack-fruit to an adolescent kiss
tongue against tongue
at a sunday evening cricket match

yellow is like that
a poui tree in blossom
golden goblets
hanging from branches

yes yellow is
that innocent
and all desire too

STAR-APPLE

purple is the color
between desire and bougainvillea
hanging over a trestle

at the funeral of an aunt
whose face i can't remember
hearing snatches of her life
that leave me wondering why
she worked herself to death

but star-apple is altogether
a different matter
as your tongue licks at
its milk-like-juice
dribbling down your chin and hands

it's knowing what you want
and not being afraid to go after him
it's the flirtatious tease before sex
at negril beach
your arms wrapped around his neck
your legs straddling his waist
and the salty sea acting as barricade

ASHAM

1

throwing back my head
i toss some in my mouth
where it lies dry on my tongue
until i salivate
and the ground corn kernels
sweetened with spices
turn paste
i swallow the treat i cherish

unlike the unexpected
visit from mister cole
when no one was home
and he asked for a glass of water
sat in the easy chair in the living room
by the window
drinking slowly

i offered to take the glass
he asked about school
said i was pretty
pulled me to sit on his lap

i felt this piece of wood squirming
as if trying to get inside of me
and i sat there breathing hard
like a dog with its tongue hanging
not hearing a word he said

i focused on his daughters
both much older than me
the oldest left his home
and came to live with us
perhaps he asked her about school
told her she was pretty
had her sit on the big stick in his lap too

hearing someone coming
he suddenly got up
hastening to tell me i was a good girl
and i wondered if i was good
because i gave him water
or sat on the wood in his lap

2

the lady who sells
asham by the school gate
sits on a crate and smiles at me
she always says i'm pretty but
she never asks me to sit on her lap
she cautions
nuh nyam too much at once
or yu will choke

taking the cone-shaped paper wrapping
i empty some in my mouth
powder up my nose
my larynx clogged

like at boston beach
when keity took me far out in the sea
and wouldn't take me back where i could stand
he held me tightly   turned me to face him
spreading my legs to straddle him
he tried to kiss me
i kept my face turned from him
then i felt his wood
forcing its way through
the leg of my bathing suit

i never told him to stop
even though i hated him

33

and when he finally took me ashore
i never went back near the water

on the beach sat a woman
selling asham
she read the terror in my eyes
called me to her and said
ah gwane teach yu how fi mek asham
first roast de corn
den shell de kernels
next grind dem with
brown sugar and add nutmeg and allspice
asham is a woman's protection

she poured some in my palm
the sweet powder
heavy on my tongue
took some of the shame from
the taste in my mouth

CARIBBEAN PASSION

i was schooled by ackee
scholar of passion
that turns the blood
a poisonous mauve
she told me one
night of purple skies

ackee is serious
about devotion
using her shirt tail
to fan the heat between her thighs

i know touch
felt it first in the sweat
that glistened on his face
my desire caught on his tongue

i sauntered the shores
my toes touched by archival script
surrounded as i am
i can't help but fondle myself

in the endless place
without seasons
there's a fruit sweeter
than star-apple's cum

ask sand
if she wearies
of waves wetting her body
swimming under her shirt

no   she shivers every time

OLEANDER

earth lying wid
she legs still spread
from de piece of loving
rain drop down pan her

same way
his guava voice
lingers in me ear
his words
aromatic oleander
dressing the road-side

the sweetness in me big
like a girl child who gets her
first bra and smiles at the feel
of her little bud
snug inside the cup

and though me don't yet know
de savor of him mouth
me know it sweet can't done
cause him eyes done
nyam-nyam me up
and words are only
mosquitoes buzzing

if you ever smell de earth
after an afternoon quickie-drench
you will understand
de tail of me feeling
nuff-nuff condensed milk
and brown-sugar sandwiched
between hard-dough bread

desire is fragrant
as pink and white oleander blossoms
and as poisonous

THIS POEM IS AN INVITATION
(for JC)

a poem is not a kiss
but you kissed
me through the telephone lines
when you read me neruda's poems

a word is not a caress
but you caressed me
with ideas and left me
hot   wet   yearning for your touch

a conversation is not benediction
but your voice resonated
beneath the layers of my skin
and i wanted you to kneel over
my body as on a prayer mat

an encounter is not commitment
but i feel my wild gallop
and i fear the calenture of your touch
this poem is an invitation

BAMBOO FINGERS

your fingers
are like slender
bamboo vines
polished to perfection
they search out
my secret places
on my breast they are padded tongs
that ignite my heat

i feel the gentle wind
pushing the bamboo vines
into a flirtatious dance
and my body sways
opening to the potion of your hands

keep stroking
i want to get lost
in the bliss of your touch
and surrender to the healing puissance
of your hands

COCONUT MAN

my tongue hungers to
trace the length of your
coconut trunk
starting from the root of your big toe
gliding slowly
savoring each particle of skin
with the flat of my tongue
until i reach your lips
where i'll savor
the coconut water quench
of your mouth
juice trickling

then when i've had my fill
i'll work my tongue down
the other side of your muscular body
resting at the swelling in your groin
i will not be a greedy eater
i'll take my time
i'll let you simmer
like coconut milk
as it boils into oil
then i'll watch you raise your hands
above your head
fingers spread like fronds
dancing in the wind
my mouth
bringing you bliss

STINKING TOE

the moment
i laid my eyes on him
i knew i should have made
a bee-line
and spared him the chase

but
i was meditating
on sin
had been reared
to eat stinking toe fruit
with its pungent smell
and hard brown skin
its meat like powder
that dissolves on touch

his smell beguiled me
but he had no meat
and never softened under
my touch

now i have
a hard brown shell
that will not be cracked

NASEBERRY

my tongue
traces your inner thigh
spilling naseberry
everywhere

your maddening sweetness
impels me
as i bite and nibble
my tongue licks your
body for more of you
to fill me
and when my fingers
press your pungent brown skin
your juices stain me

oh to be smeared
with such fruit

COCONUT

you caught me
unaware

i never suspected
when i held back my head
to drink
you would be such
a long quenching

i could not have phantomed
the delicacy of your sex
hidden in your husk's interior

i prefer you in the morning
when you are jelly soft
i open my mouth
you slide right down
my throat
my fingers stained
with your ejaculation

no wonder you
stand so tall
head in the clouds
your size a tease
for my lust

BAHIAN MAN

walking in pelourina
he hailed her
and they greeted
in the way of friends
cheek to cheek   both sides
pursed lips making a sucking sound

introduced
his triangular-shaped face and benin lips
stirred my yearning

translating
she said i was jamaican
his smile widened
and i understood
reggae music   bobmarley   rastafarians
laughter coloring his words

then he kissed me
cheek to cheek   both sides
his lips sucking at the air
and i wanted to be the breeze
caressing his lips
tall bahian man
inviting as a cup of fresh brewed coffee
steam rising from the top

i thought of all the portuguese phrases
i had practiced
how to say
i desire you

entering a local club
he at my heels

bodies pressed against bodies
i swayed to the rhythm
the fast-paced tempo of five congo drums
women with shekeres and three singers on stage

he reached for my hand
and i wanted to gulp at hot coffee
feel it scalding my tongue

he moved graceful   supple
i matched my moves to his
our bodies close
three hours later   exhausted
from a beat that never slowed
he still moved cool as snowcone
so i continued to undulate

2 a.m. people drifted
i wanted to keep dancing
he reached out
kissed me cheek-to-cheek
i tried to think
how to say
don't leave
at least not without me

he hugged me to him
whispered *ciao*
i hoped my eyes
spoke my desire eloquently
but he left me on the dance floor
wearing regret as provocatively
as i wished my words had been

NO WORD FOR THIS

yesterday
endless fields enveloped me
cane on one side
banana on the other
days stretched
no ending in sight

today
cars and sirens
meetings and appointments
and neighbors pressed in close
define my life

did i dream
the red rooster with a fat neck
that cackled every morning

i'm certain
sun-flowers grew
by my bedroom window
and my mother left my father
before i was four years old

tomorrow is a language
i'm learning to speak

CHILDHOOD LANDSCAPES

yesterday green guava nurtured me
the sun burning into the earth
sending heat-waves like a drunken waltz
staggering up into the air
heavy and scalding to the touch

doctor-birds perched on hibiscus branches
lizards with bright orange tongues catching flies
hens asleep on fences
dogs curled under the shade of houses
all trying to escape the noon day sun

getting a long stalk of cane
using my teeth to peel back the skin
licking at the juice that trickled down my chin
i'd suck on the sweet fiber until i could hear
the syrupy liquid gurgling in my stomach

red ginger flowers walled our house
beyond   the blue sea that was our mountain range
waves washing ashore
salt streaking white lines on our bodies
as we splashed   dove   never got enough
of the warm moving water

those were days that never quite ended
even when darkness finally descended
and mosquitoes clamored for the sweetness of our blood
fire-flies sang   frogs croaked and
crickets chirped in rounds under
the cotton trees with green umbrella branches

HOME

the clean smell of the earth
after rain has fallen
with the sun still prancing around
in the early afternoon

the sapphire of the sea where it meets the sky
and the tease of the river
crawling on she belly in mid august

the fecundity of mangoes in july
sweetness as abundant as spit
bounty of fruits to dazzle the eyes
cause belly-aches
& greedy flies everywhere

the yapping of dogs chasing passers-by and cars
a cow wandering lazily chewing flowers from hedge
bare-foot children running wild
their voices sailing in the wind
women in the market their legs v-spread
men pushing carts with coconuts to quench your thirst

here is were my navel-string is buried
the hue of the soil dark as me

FREEDOM

when columbus
      lost
stumbled
upon xaymaca
      the arawaks fed him

(kindness repaid
in death)

me   island daughter
nurtured with cassava soup
zemis' sweat
moistening this caribbean breeze
me umbilical cord
buried under navel-orange
me knees stained with bauxite
i am an island
hear me well
i am an island
i'll never swim too far
from these shores

SISTERS IN MISERY AND WOMANISM

I

gardens blooming
under our arms
and crotches
we were grown

we saw the way
men's eyes searched us out
and tongues
stuck out at us suggestively

we knew the meanings
behind the bold glances
saw the fear that
now draped our mothers' eyes
knew the urgency of the warnings:
let any boy touch you
you will have baby!
knew the tone of the commands
keep your dress down
and your legs closed!

we were women
every month
we went to the store
and bought our secrets
carefully concealed
in brown bags
guarded from men's eyes
but we knew they recognized
the smell of women
we knew they knew
just by the way
they looked at us

they tracked
our steps
hoping to trip us up

II

the back of our skirts
often announced
we were marked by the moon
we walked   bunched
in a circle
trying to shield
each other
certain everyone was witness
novices   want-to-be-women
we heard laughter
suffered the glares
of idle young men
the streets their stage

III

scrubbing panties
free of dried blood
was a labor to forget

walking tall
with cramps kneading our limbs
took more than will

trying to keep
the spittle that
boiled in our mouths
was often an impossibility

IV

this road
we had eagerly awaited
was unpaved
full of brambles
hormones and morals
at odds with each other

fear rather than facts
was our protection
and every month
we waited with
baited breath
for its appearance
and when it came
often inconveniently
we sighed deeply
longing for its departure

BINDING TIES

mother said
we should always
look out for and defend
each other
we sisters
caught in the crook of the sun

so we laced fingers
talking as we walked
we could be anything
knowing you cannot dig too deep
without finding water

she took the ribbon
from her hair
i doubled the waist of my skirt
legs exposed
as we thrust out our chests
and sashayed
knowing no leaf resists
the wind

mother said
never come home
without your sister
no telling what chores
you'll have to do alone

LOVE IN MY LIMBS

mosquitoes and lizards
were my playmates
darkness caressed me
and i knew the
emptiness of the
winding road
before I could spell my name

who i am
is no surprise
to those who rubbed
love into my limbs
they stamped me beautiful
willed me courage
and told me
my success was divine

I AM WHO I AM

i'm from
                a long line of women
for whom laughter was breath
women whose hands
were never idle
crocheting baking sewing
forever making something useful

                       who i am
                       is the one who would not be drowned
                       swallowing ancestors' spirits
                       that buoyed me across the atlantic

i'm from
                a long line of women
who washed clothes
and swapped stories at the river
who daily puffed out their breath
to ignite coal stoves
women who in one deft movement
wrung the neck of a chicken
that later at Sunday afternoon dinner
was seasoned so sweet

                       who i am
                       is the one that swallowed fire
                       and allowed its orange flames to dress me
                       while river mumma spat on me
                       and cooled me down

i'm from
                a long line of men
who could split a coconut
with two dexterous swings of the machete
men who knew how to grow things
and swam the ocean as eagerly
as they rode their women in the dark

54

who i am
is the pure stream of spit
on which weapons were sharpened
and medicine was measured

i'm from
                a long line of men
who took me on adventures climbing over rocks
wading through water to catch cray-fish & shrimp
men who knew the desire of a girl for a life beyond dolls and pots
uncles who took me to bars nestled in clearings
where shirtless men banged dominoes so hard the pieces flew
men who drank red-stripe and manish water
cursed as a sport
bumbo-clot their voices sang
men whose eyes said i'd soon be
a beautiful woman and claim my place
in the world
                who i am
                is not the answer but the question
                that precedes the thought
                the bulla and pear sweetness of it all

CALL ME FEMALE

i came
on a saturday
after the day
had faded
and was beckoning another
to take its place

i came
before my mother's hands
had cooled from the iron
she used to free wrinkles
from clothes

i came
at home
in the bed on which
my mother and father slept
the same bed
on which they laid and made me
with clean sheets
lightly starched and pressed

i came
quiet but certain
without prelude
or fanfare
with a head
full of hair
and a heart
as large as an air balloon

i came
with a mouth wide with noise
and my sex   heart-shaped

tucked between my legs
knowing secrets and determining
to keep them to myself

i came
female child
to a woman of twenty five years
ushered in
by a nurse's hands
friend to my mother

i came
daughter to a father
who would hoist me on his shoulders
sister to a girl
who clung to me
baby sister to brothers
who would pinch me
and kiss my cheeks
niece to aunts
who would rename me
miss madam   mother-pepper

i came
when the wind
was ripe as sweet-sop
bursting with sugar
and flowers
yawned at the adoration
piled on their beauty

i came
when the buried bone
was uncovered
and ants fought
for its forgotten juices

i came
and will keep on coming
glancing around corners
making sure
i'm still the self
i have been shaping
still the self
i'm trying to know
still the same girl
who at two
climbed to the topmost branch
of the guava tree
making her parents' hearts tremble
the same girl
who at three
found herself locked
in the maid's shower
with the neighborhood bully
the same girl
who is aunt   mother
now grandaunt

me
still coming
to unravel epithets
to claim my own

STORIES THAT SHAPE ME

i am standing
in a open field
my sister behind me

mother enjoyed stories
telling this one
her face glows
and her eyes say
that's my daughter
isn't she wonderful
isn't she brave

the stick in my hand
arrests my attention
it's at least twice my height
its weight gravitates to the ground
i clutch it with both hands
my face wears a death mask
my eyes are burning coal
the bridge of my nose
sprinkled with sweat

my mother's voice
filling in the details
always takes over here
many of the older children
in the neighborhood
were surrounding them
and that little one
she pauses
pointing to me
stood her ground
daring the gang of children
to try and take her ball and

see what she would do
with that stick

my mother's voice fades
but through the years
the constant recital
each version more embellished
moved my legs
to cross rivers   scale fences
and walk in marbled halls

MY MOTHER TO HER MOTHER

I

why was i
never the pear
you put on your bulla?

now winter
shadows my steps
i feel your unlove
like mold on my heart

in your presence
i was always a bread-fruit
splattered on the ground
belly spewing
flies buzzing

why did you throw a towel
over my head
lock me in the room
every morning
after my father left for work

why wasn't i
paradise plum
in your mouth
me the first
to call you mother

II

you withheld
your love but
your mother powdered
my body with hers

whenever she cradled me
in her lap
cupped my face
and called me her sugar baby
i saw the curtain
fall over your face

your eyes
seared my skin
as you pretended not to look
kissing your teeth
you turned away

i had what you wanted
i knew
yet my eyes smarted

III

you went to bed
and never awoke

it was my hating

you were only
thirty years old
thirty years old

three daughters
two sons
and two men
you turned your back on

all i remember
is your abhorrence

does my face
mirror yours?

my fingers itch
to wrap arms
around your neck
hear your heart sing
i love you baby
and me say
i love you too, mama

IV

mother
i deserved the orange
from the tree
not the two-day-old rind
hung to dry

you should have folded
your hands against
my father
if blame needs to be laid

you should have dug up
the yam head
and buried your compunction

you should have washed
the rancor from your eyes
boiled it with cerasee

you should have been able
to climb the hill to hold me

her grave was covered by bush
long before i was born
rats and mongooses
claimed it as a hiding place
shrub and macca encased it

but my great grand aunt says
you fava you granmuma
short same way
and peppery too

they were school-mates
and she who stood
no more then four feet nine
was the tallest of her village

she neva fraid anyone
boy or girl
no matta dem size
she would drop her
book-bag and fight

they called her miss tiny
she demanded respect
if her fist did not assault you
her tongue would bury you in the ground

darkness never kept her
from going where she needed
seemed like she welcomed it
like an illicit lover
her heart in the assurance of her hands

my mother says
she doesn't remember
my grandmother
but she is convinced
that her mother didn't like her

i suspect my mother
reminded my grandmother
too much of the independence
she traded for love
all the sweetness
souring once
her stomach began to swell

perhaps
if she hadn't died
when my mother was ten
she would have taken me
into the fields with her
would have shown me
how to wield a machete
how to plant coco
and at noon time
we would have sat
with our backs resting against a plum tree trunk
its broad leaves sheltering us
and she would have told me her dreams
would have fed them to me
with the corn-meal dumplings
and mackerel she brought for our lunch
and she would have made me promise
never to let love trick me
or be afraid of walking in the dark
she would tell me
all her secrets
but mostly
she would teach me
strength

NANNIE

you and your husband
my long deceased grandfather
waged many battles
in cuba as dressmaker and tailor
long before castro

back in jamaica working
raising two children
a son   my father
whom you cherished
and made excuses for
as if he were still
a naughty boy
the other an obedient daughter
whom you buried
when she was thirty
then raised her three daughters
and kept her widower's house

then reluctantly in the 70s
you followed son and grandchildren
to new york   braved the winter
but complained   meddled   groaned
grieved for your rented house
and idle garden in jamaica
planned always your return
but stayed and helped
raise great grandsons and daughters

nannie

edith melado palmer
melado your maiden name
remnant of the jewish ancestry
you cherished

for years i didn't remember
that you had a name

now as you lift
great grandson and daughter
into your arms
embracing me
hair silver white
and thin like a hen's
i try to
fix the details of your life
grab at the little pieces
you share reluctantly
all the stories you whispered
about susu and the things women did
with their menstrual blood to keep their men

now your eyes
look toward
100 years
and there is no wonder in your gaze
no gap in your memory
no slur in your speech
just a little hesitation in your walk

NANNIE II

skin nutmeg brown & smooth
she smelled of
baby-powder & onions
she always allowed me to crawl in her lap
would kiss me loudly
on both cheeks
her hands gentle
when she plaited my hair
and spoon-fed me
porridge every morning

later she would cry about not having
enough to give us
yet always gave us something
whenever we visited her
she knew how to measure out love
so it was never in short supply

everyone called her nannie
including my father
her voice wispy
yet when she was mad
her lips pointed like the base of a v

mostly she loved to laugh
slapping her thighs
when the joke was sweet
tears streaming down her face
she continues at ninety-eight
will not go out without her necklaces

A MEASURE OF AGE

she moved slowly
not because she couldn't walk fast
but she had lived long enough
to know no matter
the speed of the river
it will eventually meet the sea

everything in its own time
was her constant refrain
and no matter how often
i'd ask *how come?*
she'd merely shake her head and smile

when i was with her
i learned to weigh the passing of time
saw it move on its own legs
she allowed no one
to ruffle her calm
told me to stay away
from people who were always in haste
dey running from themselves
she would caution

pointing to the even-paced rhythm of nature
she showed me how to study things
slowly   with care
so to detect and relish
the beauty in all

my grandmother made me want to sprint
to become her
she made aging a timeless thing
of immense beauty
but i know
i too will eventually enjoy
a measure of age

SHE TRAVELLING

she stands
to de right
where de road forks
crooked as de mile
de crooked man
walked

hands akimbo
she legs
are firm and shiny
she hands are able
she name oman

> *bus betta mek haste and come*
> *me no have all day fi wait*

she skirt bellows up
around she ample thighs
dust swirls
eyes blink

> *but see me crosses*
> *de dust look like eh want blind me*

she basket almost topples
she hands reach up to settle
she load

> *seems like worry and crosses*
> *join friendship*

she peers
relaxes at de sound
of de bus
readies sheself
for de journey

money in me palm
food on de table

she will not sleep
in her bed for four days
night and day her place
will be in front of her
ground provisions
in a tight spot
in the market

WHAT'S IN A NAME, ASK MAROON NANNIE

fire-jumping lion
consorts
in my bosom

i am my enemy's
fire
devouring
their souls
holding back water
brimming at the river banks

in me
history dances
tales wax
answers
pathway to deliverance

herbs
render me warrior

me name
is womanself
nannie

MAROON NANNIE KNOWS DE NAME

she does wash
    all de time
        she children's clothes
        she country's poverty
        she ancestors' epitaph

she does sweep
    all de time
        cities heap wid spoils
        men's trampled manhood
        dreams swallowed by avarice

she does bruise
    all de time
        from birthing she progeny
        from de nothingness dem leave she
        from de no thanks for choosing life
        from tears used-up to douse nightmares

she does be there
    all de time
        praying but turning over soil
        lamenting de scarcity of water
        making sure trails are apparent
        and tales are memories

        when all turn irresolute
she does be there
    all de time

LIQUID BLUE TRELLIS

me eyes
neva tried
looking pan de sea

me neva know
any oder woman
wid such a long-long skirt
dat tease desire

MODA YOUNG GAL

i

because me wear low cut blouse
that accentuate me plump breasts
tight pants that hug me
sapadillo arse
and stroll down the street
sporting me poui cap
dem seh ah don't dress me age
how me should stop running
to the streets and stay home
look afta me grandchildren

eheh you see yah now
me done support four children
when dem fada was running around de place
like a one legged-man
don't get me wrong
a love me grands
but me crave more than
wet kisses and runny noses
me body yearns
for a man to hold it
like is saxophone him blowing
me body yearns
to shake to new rhythms
dance and gwane bad
like there is no tomorrow

ii

as soon as me walk pass
dem throw dem words at me back
she must think she's man

like is only man need loving
like is only man want a sweet-sweet ting
fi rub upon
why de rass people don't mind
dem own business
is fraid them fraid
fi touch themselves
but me know how fi
shut dem up
next time dem have me name in dem mouth
ah go let dem know
is yu son in me bed
de same boy whose diaper me did change
is him a lick a piece a loving pan me

ah like me men like
ah like me food
fresh and tender
me nuh inna school boys
is man me into
a man who can dance
wrap him arms round me waist
press him body into mine
a man rope tight
who whine like eel in him waist
a man whose stomach is a drum
and whose back don't ache
a man who can love
way afta de song is done

iii

him walk pass easy-easy
me feel me belly drop
me can't even begin fi trace
how we cross the age divide

but me can tell yu
how him hand vibrates
de middle of me back
how him tongue tease open
de lips of me flower
and him bring me
a bag full of laughter
instead of dutty clothes fi wash
our bodies fit
like boat pan sea
and him know how fi ride
every wave steady

me will tek all de
tongue wagging
fi wake in de arms
of a young man
and have him plant
sorrel kisses pan me
nu care how delicious
sweet-potato pudding is
it must done one day
me nah worry about
rain tomorrow when
sun hot-hot today
and me body wrap in yellow

BUMBU CLAT

yu muma bumbu clat

      in bemba
      bumama means
      sisterhood
      in jamaica
      bumbu
      is a curse
      you hurl
      going under your mother's skirt
      to shame

gu weh yu ugly
like bumba clat

      as a derivative
      bomba means to be wet or soaked
      in lingala
      bomba connotes hiding

      before pads and tampons
      women used cloth napkins
      left them soaking in basins
      (covered and concealed)
      to bleach out the blood

yu is nutten but
a little bumbu clat

      as a teenager
      whenever i had to purchase
      pads i waited
      until no one else
      was in line
      then i made sure they
      were carefully wrapped
      tucked under my arm

goweh bumbu clat

>monthly mortality
>spills from between
>our legs
>but a woman's blood
>can bind long after
>lust is weary
>
>who then will understand
>the song that rumbles
>in your groin
>the ache that is a lover's
>meditation

wha de bumbu clat
yu do   is mad yu mad

>unless anansism is your guise
>you'll not be able to trick the snake
>to victory
>but bumba as verb
>creates a space
>out of unease

what a bumbu clat

>a male word
>that wets the tongue
>denouncing and advertising
>the taboo and craving

ah gwane mash up
yu bumbu clat

>always the instinct
>to make you a splattered sweet-sop
>white meat with black seeds
>juice leaking on the ground

BANDA

in the graveyard
where we straddle
life and death
dancing banda
caressing our bodies
a time of fecund
possibility
with top hat and bow-tie
we thrust
and prance
old and crippled
virile and debauched

locked in the moment
abandonment rules
sweat scents
the droaning of the drums
devours our appetites

the ground braces
and gives us back
our cry for life

in this mid-way point
between then and now
we dance
calling life
waving to death
decay and fertility

let the ash from
the cigar singe
your skin

move to the drum
       don't stop until
             the casse signals

    banda   dance
        banda   prance

    dance death to dust

    dance life to sunrise

SKY-JUICE

everywhere
the smell of the sea
blends with fear
everywhere
burglar bars
shut out tropical ease
jewelry locked away in chests
car windows rolled up
locking out the breeze

everywhere
confusion
every where
the struggle
to survive
rasta brethren
standing by half-way-tree
hawking woollen tams
higglers' wares
blocking entrances to stores

everywhere
the desire for escape
as de sound blares
from record shops
where rude boys
step left
shuffle right
or in de juke joints
whe dem lean against walls
one hand holding a redstripe
de other guarding dem balls
eyes lost in paradise
or dem hangout at the disco

on thursday night
oldies but goodies
rent-a-tile with someone
other than your wife

everywhere
is people begging
wash yu windshield fah you ma'am
boys selling the *evening star*
darting between
the after work traffic

everywhere
mad people
walk and talk
to themselves
accosting motorists
and pedestrians
streaking when de
spirit tek dem

everywhere
reminders of a different past
pocomania worshippers
in white frocks with blue sashes
call on the spirits
africa in their steps

every day
too many people
are stuffed
into the mini buses
and someone is killed
trying to get from home to work

every day
the gap widens
foreign consumption escalates

the haves grumble
bout the three v's
video   vulva   visa
jump on an air jamaica taxi
to shop in miami

every day
people go mad
under the heat
every day
the anthem is still
them belly full
but we hungry

NUH GLORY IN POVATI

all dem book people
deh write bout
we plight
but nuh a dem
ave any solution
fi right de wrong

all dem book people
write bout dem need
fi study de situation
tek first hand account
gwane like dere
is glory in
dis povati
dat we who is mostly
black   mostly ex-slaves
(me know seh is not only black people)
suffa unda

well mek me
tell all ah oonuh
good intentional intellectual
seems to me
is de rich need studying
and writing bout
why dem have so much
and still dig out we eye
why dem waste so much
den look pan we wid disdain
study de rich
why dem pockets bulging
study de barclay banks
de shell & exxon

de imf executives
de kaiser aluminum
and diamond traders

study why
de rougher we hand
de less we mek
and is we keeping the world
clean and fed

so nuh ask me nuh question
bout dis povati
since you book people
have so much time
pan oonuh hand
tell we how fi get
some dunny

BOAT PEOPLE

(for the people of haiti who survived the sea)

damballa   damballa
damballa oh

oldman   gatekeeper
i see you eclipsed
by the light of day
your silhouette hangs
like a dress caught on a nail

where are your eyes oldman
what has happened to your hands?
on the back of a horse
you merge
not animal   not man
a power surging through the wind
fire sweeping at your heels

open the gate oldman
hold back the waves   gatekeeper

damballa   damballa
damballa oh

every time we move
we move with water
every time we move
the voyage
identifies us
like the hue of our skin
every time we fight
we shame the enemy
who tries to drown us
uses water to embalm us

freedom or death
toussaint sounds the abeng
freedom not death
christophe rattles the shell
freedom and liberty
dessaline rides the wind

salt water spews
from between our legs
killing the gangrene in our
slaving souls
bursting the boils
devouring the insides
of our children's mouths
freedom never death
we shame the enemy

oldman   gatekeeper
i see you in the middle
of the crossroads
standing on one leg
the other amputated in flight
your staff a pole
cemented to the ground
you're the people   white-cane
tapping on the water
neither male nor female
the people
with voices knocking
in their heads
who remember other promises
know the material
to weave dreams

olodumare   ancestral spirit
always water
salty waves

damballa   damballa
damballa oh

oldman   gatekeeper
where to find refuge?
we gather our lives like shells
and flee in boats
that crabs know
not to trust
we are not eels
and when our tied-together rafters
rupture in the ocean
we are swallowed
or washed ashore
like jellyfish

after all the planning
after all the blood
after all the burning
for liberty not starvation
we are without a home
toussaint betrayed
to die in a french prison
color and class divided
invaded and infected
with corruption
our freedom a prize rescinded
the glory not yet ours

oldman
your tears leave a trail
that fat red ants fight over
but the meat is dry
your feet bruise the earth
iguanas wrap their stomachs
and the sand is stink with memory

but as our voices
ricochet from the waves
the drums sound

damballa   damballa
damballa oh

our irresistible spirits flare

damballa   damballa
damballa oh

THOSE WHO DIDN'T MAKE IT

they believed
with faith they would walk
like the blue-eyed
patriarch they venerated
didn't the water ferment itself
and hold him up?
> *ayibobo*
>> *tete ensemm*
> *ayibobo*
>> *pale*

the sea done rise up
muscles wrung like rope
steer and grip
the make-shift boat
clutching the splintering board
> *ayibobo*
> *ayibobo*

blood does not run here
death does not dance here
> *ayibobo*
> *ayibobo*

a woman
face down
one arm pinned
to her side

a young man
ready to claim wife
floats   mouth full of fish

a wife's fingers
cuffs the angular wrist of her child
determined to save him

a sister
desiring to lay eyes
on her only living relatives
clutches a cloth in her fist

a man   a believer
beaten near death
by the tonton macoutes
bluish-black face
glistens   water gurgling
from his mouth

two first cousins
trapped but not delivered
by sea-weed

a mother of five
raped   teeth knocked out
is pulled under then belched up

an orphaned ten year old boy
floats in his birth clothes

a young woman aged in the barren fields
and tyrant sun since age nine
bounces up and down
diamond water frames her face

a little girl
weighted down by waves
except for her red ribbon
braided in her tight plaits

those with name
who will become the nameless
        ayibobo
        ayibobo
                tet ensemm
                tet ensemm

for the rest
the salty miami beach
disperses them
but the journey won't end
   ayibobo
the sea done rise up
a skyscraper
pushing them down
swallowing them
into its endless mouth
reuniting them
with the inveterate wails
they had not until now
understood

   ayibobo   *ayibobo*   *ayibobo*
   tet ensemm

de sea done rise up
bumbu-cloth
curses of our mothers' betrayal
washes them ashore
semen staining their legs
propagating more
for the migration

   ayibobo
   ayibobo

      liberte
      tet ensemm
      liberte
      tet ensemm

SUMMER RAINS

heat wraps its tentacles
around the face
exiles the yearning
to go about

as mangoes   belly-round
bloated as a shark washed ashore
lie mutilated
by wheels in the street

hurricane loafs atop
orange-red flamboyant trees
tossing petals on the heads
of passers-by

lightning hangs low
as water cascades like lava
distorting
the ache in the tooth

spirits live here
in the mid-day rain
raising the heat to suffocation
in the curves of palm trees

coiling the natural energy
into a circle
iguanas
eat from their hands

clapping thunder
frightens awake the brain
pacified by the air-
conditioner's hum

the native deity
dances fiercely
and invites shango
to dine

but hurricane isn't somnolent
he watches all
out-waiting
some moment's inattention

HEAD IN IDEA

(for Kamau Brathwaite)

is man dat

him dere
walking wid him head
in idea

is how him come so
dat man dere
him lips mouthing
words we ain't think of yet
but which we live?

always him eyes
lost in clouds of words
buried deep in de connotations
plowin through de puns and wordplay
scatterin de lexicon from de root
dat man dere

is how him come
de poet of we heart
dat sweet man
who speak
like him know fah true
dat him words
is de handkerchief
we been seekin fi wipe
de tears from we eye?

is who put dem words
in him mouth?
he who always

talkin wid
him words pounding
like hurricane wind
him words ebbin and flowin
like de waves
him words stars
in de sky lightin a dark night

yes him
de man
who eyes ain't seein
only what is happenin
but what makes it happen
who knows how to make it happen
another way
so we not always on de bottom
bearing the brunt of de weight

dat man
me heart did embrace
long time
dis poet of de people
dis wordsmith
dis lover of idea and language
who remind we dat
is more dan one way
fi skin de rabbit
is more dan one tongue
we have to speak
how we mus ban we belly and bawl
holler and claim we humanity
how we need fi rejoice

so me steady watchin him
me steady listenin to wha him seh
me steady learnin him words

and writin me own
because me wan dat man
walkin wid him head
enshrined in ideas
fi know me well groovin on what him seh
me long time now a rub-a-dub
mellowin on him words
me long time a romance him
poet of de people

SPANISH TOWN

is more than twenty years
me been on dis same street
that is like boy pickinie
that outgrow him short pants
me see and know it all
me have a corner of this market
nowadays me a pedal
american grapes
green and purple
and foreign carrots
fat and sweet

tek it easy an watch whe yu ah guh
me ahfi call to the nice lady
a try run in her spike heel shoes

move out de way!
an mind de crazy motorists
knock yu down
me holler to de little girl
a skip and sing like she inna her yard

beg excuse
and step around nuh
me screw up me face
and remind de youth
bout manners which
me sure him muma teach him

how it ah guh? yu looking well nice
me nuff up to the church sister
who always buy from me

yu tink yu own de road
is nuh yu one have some whe fi guh yu know
is dead yu wan kill people
everyday dem mini-bus
drive like them mad and
dem cyan dead too

gu weh yu ugly like spite
dis same nasty man
piss by de side where
people must walk everyday
damn nogood beast

she mus tink she is mango pan tree
in dose yellow shoes and green dress

well is time me close
dis little shop

jah rastafari

walk good

FI ME PEOPLE

(for fay, kezia, eddy, guichard, myriam, danielle, sheryl & donna)

fi me people
cinnamon brown to coffee black
nutmeg tint to copper tone
carrying de smell of cane-fields
nyaming green bananas dem tally
for foreign felicity
seasoning all dem eat wid
coconut milk
various   hopeful people

fi me people
playing jacks and cricket
gathering for ring games and soccer matches
transforming de stick fight
into dance
burying dem orishas
behind white saints
holding ground
most of de time
dem eyes elsewhere
dan de immediate squalor
others would have dem
accept as dem life
exultant   transcending people

fi me people
shut out and hustling
in negril & cross-roads
port a spain & laventille
port a prince & lemonade
curacao & aruba
san juan & loiza

bathing in buckets
washing clothes at de river
or de stand-pipe
nightly rinsing
de one school uniform
so dat each morning de pickney dem
clean & freshly pressed
hard-working   resilient people

fi me people
keeping dem ancestors close
putting out food
for de duppies & santos
who dream and guide dem
through trouble and bad-mindedness
sprinkling salt for de soucouyant
guarding de children
from lougawou
sharpening and raising
de machetes and cutlass
in work and defense
resting come noon day
under de zabricot   mango
flamboyant trees
immoveable   rooted people

fi me people
speaking kringlish   spanglish
papiamento   creole
inventing new tongues
chatting all de time
reciting and retelling
dem stories
dancing de bomba   plena
moving to de voodun drums
reggae beat   calypso pulse

refusing to be subsumed
determined to mek dem
lives an example
inventive   tenacious people

fi me people
wid dem plenty laugh
and good-good time selves
wid touchy-touchy hands
dat always connect wid life
dispossessed maligned
nigger-spirited souls
from ghana to south carolina
jamaica to nigeria
haiti to alabama
cuba to st john
fi me people
dem palms touch mine
warm and loving
raising me to me feet
singing me home
giving me back meself
fi love

ABOUT THE AUTHOR

Opal Palmer Adisa is a Jamaica-born, award-winning poet, educator and storyteller. Her poetry, stories and articles have been anthologized widely.

She is the co-founder of Watoto Wa Kuumba, a children's theatre group that she directed from 1979-1991. Since 1993, Opal Palmer Adisa has taught literature and served as Chair of the Ethnic Studies/ Cultural Diversity Program at the California College of Arts and Crafts in Oakland.

Her published works include: *Leaf-of-Life*, poetry, Jukebox Press, 2000; *It Begins With Tears*, novel, Heinemann, 1997; *Tamarind and Mango Women*, poetry, Sister Vision Press, 1992; *traveling women*, poetry, Jukebox Press, 1989; *Bake-Face and Other Guava Stories*, Kelsey Street Press, 1986; *Pina, The Many-Eyed Fruit*, children's book, Julian Richardson Press, 1985

Over 140 Caribbean, Black British and South Asian titles can be bought on Peepal Tree's website on a secure server:
www.peepaltreepress.com or by mail order from:
Peepal Tree Press, 17 King's Avenue, Leeds LS6 1QS
Telephone: (+44) 0113 245 1703 2
Email: hannah@peepaltreepress.com